LIFE AT WINTERTHUR:
A DU PONT FAMILY ALBUM

BY MAGGIE LIDZ

copyright page:

To Franz

The author thanks Neville Thompson and Pauline Eversmann at Winterthur for their ongoing support and thanks Heather Clewell, Winterthur's archivist, and Marge McNinch and Barb Hall at Hagley Museum. She also appreciates Ruth Lord Holmes, P. L. Harrison, John A. H. Sweeney, William (Mike) du Pont, and Anna Glen Vietor for sharing their unique perspectives. Special thanks to editor Lisa Lock, photographer Herb Crossan, and designer Suzanne Gaadt.

All photographs courtesy Winterthur Archives, except: 2, 3 (portrait), 4, 5 (left), 6 (bottom), 7 (background), 9 (top), 10 (top), 11, 13 (drawings), 14 (left), 18 (bottom), 19 (background, bottom left and right), 20 (invitation), 21 (middle and bottom), 28 (drawing), 38 (portrait), 51 (invitation); all courtesy of Hagley Museum and Library.

credits:

Editor: Lisa L. Lock

Designer: Suzanne DeMott Gaadt, Gaadt Perspectives, LLC

Printer: Innovation Printing and Lithography, Inc.

Library of Congress Cataloging-in-Publication Data

Lidz, Maggie, 1958–
    Life at Winterthur : a Du Pont family album / Maggie Lidz.
        p. cm.
    ISBN 0-912724-56-0
    1. Du Pont family. 2. Henry Francis du Pont Winterthur Museum. 3. Winterthur (Del.)--Biography. I. Henry Francis du Pont Winterthur Museum. II. Title.
    CT274.D87 L53 2001 Oversice
    975.1'1--DC21

                    2001004273

LIFE AT WINTERTHUR: A DU PONT FAMILY ALBUM

By Maggie Lidz

chapters:

INTERTHUR WAS A HOME IN THE MOST FUNDAMENTAL MEANING OF THE WORD—IN AN EMOTIONAL SENSE. WINTERTHUR WAS THE FAMILY SEAT, AND IT REMAINED THE SETTING FOR ALL SPECIAL OCCASIONS: CHRISTMAS, EASTER, WEDDINGS, AND EXTRAVAGANT HOUSE PARTIES.

INTRODUCTION

>>This family album chronicles life at the place the du Pont family called home for more than a century—Winterthur. Babies were born there, children grew up there, young people were married there, old people died there. Their story begins in 1874, the year that the Winterthur estate was given to Henry Algernon du Pont as a wedding present, and ends in 1951, on the eve of a new beginning for Winterthur as a public building, the focal point of what is today Winterthur Museum, Garden & Library.

Five weddings spanning three generations are recounted in this book, celebrating love, family, and the future. Yet the house at Winterthur was a stage for tragedy as well: the deaths of children, the loss of a mother, a broken engagement. The lives of the people who lived at Winterthur were as interwoven with happiness and pain as life is anywhere.

The records of the development of the house and grounds are carefully preserved in the Archives at Winterthur. Ninety-six filing cabinets of personal letters, children's drawings, tradesmen's bills, staff memoranda, newspaper clippings, and personal account books—70 years worth—contain everything from receipts for a single order of dog food to hundreds of architectural blueprints. The household management system responsible for preserving this wealth of information was established at Winterthur in the early 20th century. At the top of the managerial pyramid was the owner, Henry Algernon du Pont, and

later his son, Henry Francis. The division supervisors for the house, farm, and greenhouses worked closely with the owner and kept careful accounts of their responsibilities. And the du Pont children had an entirely separate and autonomous division of nurses, tutors, and governesses. Private secretaries took dictation and filed copies of every piece of paper that was sent in or out of Winterthur.

The records generated by this system allow us to glimpse the evolution of the estate and the lives of the people who called it home. Winterthur was the only residence of Henry Algernon and his family. Most of the family's time and money was spent there. But the seemingly limitless wealth generated by the expansion of the DuPont company at the end of World War I allowed his son, Henry Francis, and his family to use Winterthur in a wholly different manner. Winterthur became the anchor to a life spent seasonally circulating among other family houses: a New York apartment, a Southampton summer home, and a Florida bungalow compound. But Winterthur was a home in the most fundamental meaning of the word—in an emotional sense. Winterthur was the family seat, and it remained the setting for all special occasions: Christmas, Easter, weddings, and extravagant house parties.

We invite you in for a glimpse of Winterthur as seen through the eyes of the du Pont family. The many never-before-published photographs and personal reminiscences on the following pages record the public and private aspects of life at one of America's grand old country estates.

chapter 1

"HER SWEET FACE":
THE 1874 WEDDING

Colonel Henry Algernon du Pont, ca. 1865

>>On a sweltering day in New York City, July 15, 1874, Pauline Foster married Colonel Henry Algernon du Pont, scion of the wealthy du Pont family of Delaware. Pauline was an orphan and had been without a permanent home since her father died five years before, but she brought an income of her own and a secure social standing to the marriage. The Colonel's tightly knit and well-settled clan must have charmed her as much as the seriousness of his intentions and his illustrious Civil War record.

"THE WEDDING WOULD HAVE BEEN DELIGHTFUL AND A PERFECT SUCCESS IF IT HAD NOT BEEN FOR THE EXCESSIVE HEAT. EVEN WITH THIS DRAWBACK WE ALL ENJOYED IT IMMENSELY... PAULINE LOOKED LOVELY IN HER WEDDING DRESS AND HER SWEET FACE HAS BEEN BEFORE ME EVER SINCE."

—LOUISA GERHARD DU PONT TO HER SON, HENRY ALGERNON (JULY 27, 1874)

The wedding took place at a fashionable Fifth Avenue church. Attended by six bridesmaids, Pauline wore a lace veil and a white silk dress looped with silk jasmine blossoms. Wedding presents were laid out in a glittering array of porcelain, bronze, gold, and silver. Pauline's record book of wedding gifts begins with a silver soup tureen and ends with bronze candlesticks. The Colonel gave his wife diamond and pearl earrings, but the most extravagant present is not listed in Pauline's gift book. The Colonel's parents had given the couple a new home—Winterthur.

Pauline Foster in her wedding dress, 1874

THESE SILK FLOWERS FROM

PAULINE'S WEDDING DRESS

HAVE BEEN SAVED IN THE

ARCHIVES AT WINTERTHUR.

"THE MANTLE PIECES WERE COVERED WITH

FLOWERS LAID CLOSE TOGETHER SO AS TO HIDE THE

MARBLE SHELF. PAULINE'S FRIENDS (ALL WHO COULD NOT COME) HAD SENT HER BOUQUETS

AND BASKETS OF FLOWERS UNTIL THE WHOLE TOP OF THE PIANO WAS COVERED WITH THEM.

ALL THE MOST LOVELY TEA-ROSES, HELIOTROPE, EXOTICS..."

—LOUISA GERHARD DU PONT, PAULINE'S MOTHER-IN-LAW,

TO ELEUTHERA DU PONT SMITH (JULY 28, 1874)

Life at Winterthur: A du Pont Family Album

chapter 2

Winterthur:
The Wedding Present

Winterthur, ca. 1874

>>Pauline paid her first visit to Winterthur in August 1874. Her husband "showed her the spring & ferns & all the lovely wood paths around the house." Her first thoughts were about furnishing her new residence: "If we only get all the fancy things safely to Winterthur," Pauline wrote to her sister, "our house will be charming."

The Colonel knew Winterthur intimately, having spent many happy hours there as a child. In 1874 the rural Delaware estate consisted of 445 acres of farmland and woods anchored by a 12-room, 1839 Greek-revival villa. The Colonel's aunt Evelina du Pont and her husband, Jacques Antoine Bidermann, had spent the last 20 years of their lives developing the property into a showplace of scientifically managed farms and flower-filled gardens. The Bidermanns' tenanted gatehouse guarded a mile-long drive to the residence. Inside the stone-walled boundaries were spacious barns, orchards, a greenhouse, and a formal rose garden.

Evelina died at Winterthur in 1863. After Antoine died in 1865, their son, who lived in Paris, sold the estate to his uncle Henry du Pont, who bought it with the intention of giving it to one of his children. The Colonel, his firstborn, was the lucky recipient.

"Winterthur... I earnestly hope our dear Pauline will like it and you will have many years of happiness there together."

—Louisa Gerhard du Pont to her son, Henry Algernon (July 27, 1874)

chapter 3

HENRY AND PAULINE

Pauline Foster (*first on the left in the frame*) with friends, ca. 1870

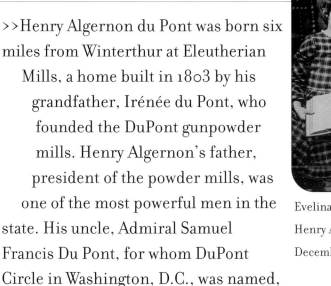

Evelina, Ellen Eugenia, and Henry Algernon du Pont, December 1849

>>Henry Algernon du Pont was born six miles from Winterthur at Eleutherian Mills, a home built in 1803 by his grandfather, Irénée du Pont, who founded the DuPont gunpowder mills. Henry Algernon's father, president of the powder mills, was one of the most powerful men in the state. His uncle, Admiral Samuel Francis Du Pont, for whom DuPont Circle in Washington, D.C., was named, inspired Henry Algernon to pursue a military career. Graduating first in his class at West Point in 1861, he later received a Congressional Medal of Honor for his "most distinguished gallantry" during the terrible Battle of Cedar Creek. The Colonel, as he was known for the rest of his life, met his future wife in Newport, Rhode Island, where he was in command of Fort Adams and she was on vacation in the elegant resort town.

The vivacious Pauline Foster made a dazzling impression on the rather sober and sometimes overly earnest Colonel du Pont. Her mother had died 10 days after her birth, and her father, Henry Ten Eyck Foster, a much-respected gentleman farmer from a prosperous, old New York family, died in 1869 when Pauline was 20. Orphaned, she and her older brother, Antoine Lentilhon ("Lenty"), and sister, Anna, sold the family farm and journeyed together on a Grand Tour of Europe. Upon their return, they became attractive figures in the New York social whirl, using their grandmother's Manhattan brownstone as a base to travel from country house to country house, resort to resort, as the season and invitations dictated.

> "*I* HOPE IN THAT SOME TIME YOU MAY SEND ME AN ANSWER TO MY LETTER, TELLING ME ABOUT SOME OF THE JOLLY THINGS YOU HAVE SEEN & DONE SINCE THAT MEMORABLE FOURTH OF JULY WHEN WE THREW TORPEDOES AT COLONEL DU PONT'S HAT & SET OFF FIRECRACKERS IN THE RAIN!"
> —EDITH WHARTON TO HER FRIEND, PAULINE DU PONT (SEPTEMBER 23, 1874)

chapter 4

A Paris
HONEYMOON

>>The Colonel and Pauline spent a year honeymooning in Europe. The extended trip, while not unusual among Pauline's New York acquaintances, was a little unnerving to the Colonel's relations, who had traveled to Europe before but not at such a leisurely pace or for no other purpose than pleasure. The usually taciturn Colonel wrote to his father that Paris was a "beautiful city which had far exceeded all the antici-pations I had formed." But although the couple had a "perfect admiration for everything French," they were thinking of Winterthur and spent much of their time buying furnishings for their Delaware home. Everything from egg boilers and saucepans to carpets, upholstered furniture, antique textiles, Chinese porcelain vases, carved sideboards, and bronze stat-uettes were purchased abroad.

Portrait of the Colonel taken in
Paris, 1874 – 75

Portrait of Pauline taken in Paris, 1874 – 75

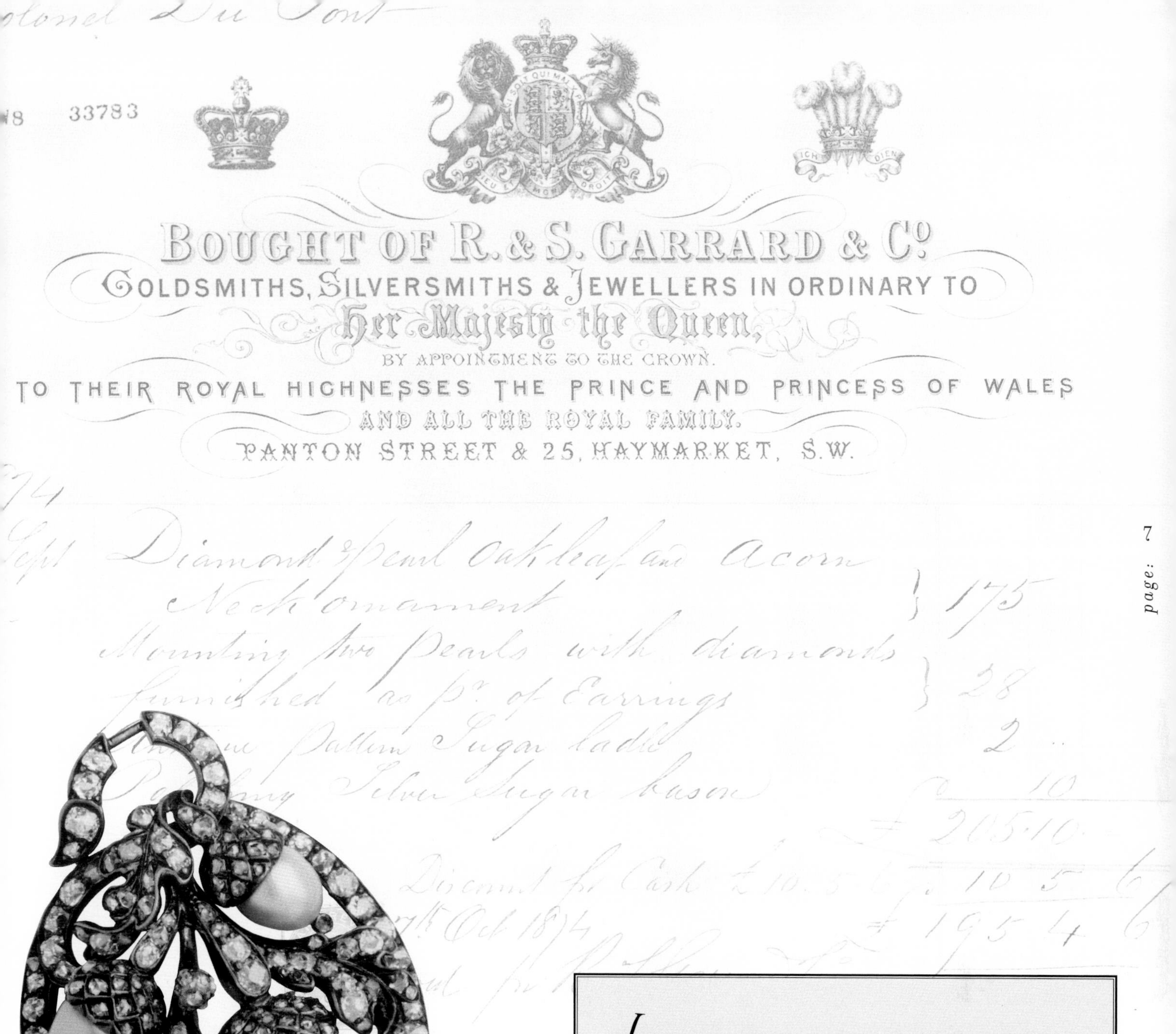

BOUGHT OF R. & S. GARRARD & Cº.
GOLDSMITHS, SILVERSMITHS & JEWELLERS IN ORDINARY TO
Her Majesty the Queen,
BY APPOINTMENT TO THE CROWN.

TO THEIR ROYAL HIGHNESSES THE PRINCE AND PRINCESS OF WALES
AND ALL THE ROYAL FAMILY.
PANTON STREET & 25, HAYMARKET, S.W.

Colonel Du Pont

N8   33783

[handwritten ledger]

74

Sept   Diamond & Pearl Oak leaf & Acorn
         Neck ornament   175

         Mounting two Pearls with diamonds
         furnished as pr. of Earrings   28

         ...Fine Pattern Sugar ladle   2 ..

         ...my Silver Sugar bason   ..   10

                                                     205.10.

         Discount for Cash £10.5.6   10 5 6

         7th Oct 1874   195 4 6

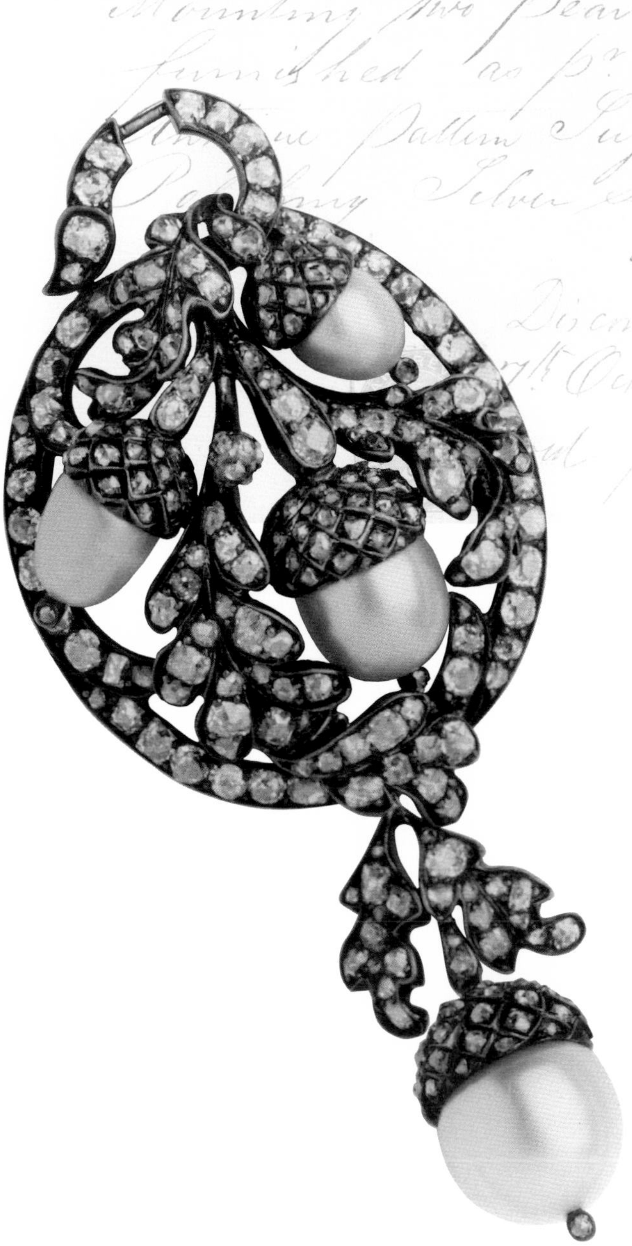

> "*I* BOUGHT MY PRESENT THE OTHER DAY FROM UNCLE
> GIRAUD AND IT IS BEAUTIFUL—PEARLS AND BRILLIANTS
> SET IN SILVER, A BUNCH OF OAK LEAVES AND ACORNS, VERY
> PRACTICAL AND VERY HANDSOME. IT DID NOT TAKE ALL MY
> MONEY SO I WILL HAVE ENOUGH LEFT TO BUY A PEARL
> NECKLACE WHICH I HAVE ALWAYS WANTED... HENRY IS
> GOING TO HAVE MY EARRINGS RESET LIKE THE PENDANT SO
> I WILL HAVE A BEAUTIFUL SET."
>
> —PAULINE DU PONT TO
> HER SISTER, ANNA (SEPTEMBER 25, 1874)

Life at Winterthur: A du Pont Family Album

chapter 5

THE
FIRSTBORN

>>The du Ponts' first child was born in Paris on April 2, 1875. Named Cathérine Barthélémie Pauline after Pauline's maternal great-grandmother, the adoring parents called her Paulinette.

Cathérine Barthélémie
Pauline du Pont, 1875

M Y DEAR MAMA ALTHOUGH I CANNOT YET WRITE WITH PEN AND INK I THOUGHT YOU WOULD LIKE A NOTE IN PENCIL TO TELL YOU A LITTLE OF YOUR WONDERFUL GRANDDAUGHTER, FOR AS YOU SAY, HENRY'S DESCRIPTION IS NOT TO BE TRUSTED. I ONLY WISH YOU COULD SEE THE DEAR LITTLE CREATURE YOURSELF. SHE IS SO SWEET & CUNNING WITH THE ROUNDEST OF LITTLE CHEEKS, BLUE EYES, VERY RATHER RETROUSSÉ. LIGHT HAIR AND NOT VERY MUCH OF IT, A DOUBLE CHIN AND RATHER A GOOD SIZED MOUTH. EVERY ONE SAYS SHE LOOKS LIKE HENRY AND INSTEAD OF HIS FEELING VERY MUCH HONORED HE SAYS HE DOESN'T THINK IT AT ALL A COMPLIMENT. THE BABY MADE THE FIRST APPEARANCE ON THE CHAMPS-ELYSÉES YESTERDAY AND SHE HAS JUST GONE AGAIN TODAY SO THAT SHE HAS GOTTEN QUITE THE START OF HER MAMAN WHO HAS BEEN RATHER TOO WEAK TO TRY THAT YET—WE WEIGHED THE BABY LAST TUESDAY AND FOUND SHE HAD GAINED TWO POUNDS IN A MONTH, WHICH THEY SAY IS DOING VERY WELL. YOU REALLY CAN SEE HER GROW AND I AM SURE THERE IS EVERY REASON SHE SHOULD. FOR THE MOST OF HER TIME IS SPENT EATING. THE REST IS SLEEPING AND EXERCISING HER LUNGS, WHICH WE CAN ALL TESTIFY ARE STRONG, AND IN A FAIR WAY OF BECOMING STRONGER IF PRACTICE HAS ANY EFFECT. PLEASE TELL ME IF HENRY SQUEALED MUCH IN HIS YOUTHFUL DAYS, I HOPE HE DID.

—PAULINE DU PONT TO HER MOTHER-IN-LAW, LOUISA GERHARD (MAY 6, 1875)

chapter 6

Coming
Home

Eleutherian Mills, ca. 1870

>>In October of 1875, the little family of three finally sailed for home. They were accompanied by Philippine Veyssier, a young French woman engaged to care for Paulinette. Setting up a house was a laborious business in those days, and it was decided that the first winter would be spent with the Colonel's parents at Eleutherian Mills. Paulinette, "sweet & lovely, so blooming, the image of health & strength," charmed her grandparents. The Colonel went to work in his father's office, and Pauline and Philippine, with the eager assistance of the Colonel's mother and his sisters, cared for the baby and prepared to move into Winterthur in the spring.

"I AM GLAD MY DEAR PAULINE, TO THINK THAT YOU ARE COMING TO YOUR COUNTRY HOME BEFORE ITS AUTUMN BEAUTY HAS PASSED AWAY. THE WOODS ARE STILL FULL OF FLOWERS, FRINGED GENTIANS, ASTERS AND GOLDEN RODS BRIGHT WITH THEIR GOLD AND CRIMSON DYES."

—LOUISA GERHARD DU PONT TO HER DAUGHTER-IN-LAW, PAULINE (OCTOBER 23, 1875)

chapter 7

MOURNING

Sophie Madeline du Pont, Henry Algernon's aunt, sent this condolence book to Pauline.

Henry Algernon and Pauline's children's tombstones in the du Pont family cemetery

>> Life was tranquil until March, when Paulinette became suddenly and seriously ill one month before her first birthday. She died on March 5, 1876.

Tragically, this child's death was the first of many for the couple. Pauline bore six more children between 1877 and 1885, only two of whom survived: the robust Louise Evelina, born August 3, 1877, and the more delicate Henry Francis, born May 27, 1880.

A son, Antoine Irénée, had been born June 18, 1879, but had died the same day. Twin boys were born two years after Henry Francis, and their grand-mother was enchanted: "They are wrapped in cotton flannels with bottles of warm water around them. You can't imagine any thing prettier & sweeter than they are lying together in the same bed, they have regular features & dark hair and eyes."

Pierre, the weaker of the two, died after two fitful days. The more vigorous twin, Paul, died at six months. Their last child, Anna, was considered "lovely, strong & well" right up until the day before she died of croup at seven months on February 26, 1886. Church attendance and charitable work became Pauline's solace during 10 difficult years of pregnancy, childbirth, and mourning.

> "POOR PAULINE HAS BEEN <u>VERY</u> WEAK SINCE THE DEATH OF HER BABY... [BUT SHE] BEARS ALL LIKE A TRUE CHRISTIAN, & SO UNSELFISH & FULL OF KIND THOUGHT FOR OTHERS.... POOR HENRY SEEMS TO SUFFER MORE THAN HER EVEN, IT IS SUCH A CRUEL BLOW TO HIM; HE FEELS <u>FOR HER</u> TOO AS WELL AS HIMSELF— HE DOTED ON HER LITTLE ONE."
>
> —SOPHIE MADELINE DU PONT, HENRY ALGERNON'S AUNT, TO A FRIEND (MARCH 8, 1876)

chapter 8

THE NEW HOME

"WE HAVE BEEN IN OUR HOUSE NOW FOR ABOUT TWO MONTHS AND OF COURSE HAVE BEEN VERY BUSY, I INSIDE THE HOUSE AND MY HUSBAND OUT OF DOORS. THERE WERE SO MANY TREES AROUND THE HOUSE THAT WE HAVE HAD A GREAT MANY CUT, WHICH IS A GREAT IMPROVEMENT. THE WOODS ARE BEAUTIFUL AND FILLED WITH BERRIES, AND SEVERAL SPRINGS."

—PAULINE DU PONT TO HER COUSIN (JUNE 30, 1876)

>>The move to the newly renovated house, only weeks after the death of Paulinette, was difficult: "We had looked forward with so much pleasure to coming here with her," Pauline wrote to her cousin wistfully, "She would have made our house so bright & happy." Paulinette's nurse, Philippine Veyssier, had stayed on with the couple, working as a chambermaid and seamstress. A young Irish girl was hired as kitchen help, and a farmer's daughter from Pennsylvania was the cook. The du Ponts were good employers, and many of the people who worked at Winterthur remained a long time. John Wesley Chapple worked as superintendent of the Winterthur Farms for 40 years. August Dauphin, a native of France, was hired as the butler before 1900 and remained until his death in 1917.

Winterthur, ca. 1875–76

LOUISE AND HARRY

Louise and Henry Francis du Pont, ca. 1882

>>The Colonel and Pauline were exceptionally devoted parents to their two surviving children. Cared for by the attentive Philippine, Louise and Henry (nicknamed Harry) spent a happy childhood roaming the estate, observing nature. Not surprisingly, Harry and Louise remained close their entire lives. A cousin from New York, Sally Nicholson Elliot, recalled those days at Winterthur in a letter to Louise:

Winterthur's train station

I have been thinking of the old days…. Were you too young to remember the first time the train passed Winterthur? We all got up from the table & rushed to the window, you had hold of my hand & you jumped up & down & shouted for joy. How well I remember the house as it was then, and your mother serving the soup out of the lovely soup tureen. Harry didn't like soup so I remember the words "mange la soup" being said to him till the last drop was down.

Louise and Henry Francis with Philippine
Veyssier, ca. 1884

"THE CHILDREN ARE WELL & LAST TUESDAY HARRY CEL-
EBRATED HIS 4TH BIRTHDAY BY HAVING 11 LITTLE COUSINS
TO SPEND THE AFTERNOON WITH HIM. I AM MAKING GREAT
EFFORTS TO TEACH HIM YET HE EVIDENTLY IS NOT FOND OF
BOOKS. LOUISE IS DEVOTED TO THEM… AND FOR THE LAST
YEAR HAS READ PERFECTLY IN ANY FRENCH BOOK. SHE HAS
TAUGHT HERSELF TO READ IN ENGLISH."

PAULINE DU PONT TO HER HUSBAND'S COUSIN,
CAMILLE BIDERMANN (JULY 1, 1884)

Louise was a prolific artist
as a child, filling notebooks
with small sketches.

Life at Winterthur: A du Pont Family Album

chapter 10

THE WINTER HOLIDAYS

Harry and Louise's mother, Pauline, was also a collector. These costume cards she gathered and saved are now in the Archives at Winterthur.

>> Harry and Louise shared their parents' passion for collecting. But rather than family manuscripts and heirloom furniture, the children amassed stamps, pennies, birds' eggs, and greeting cards. Their collection of 1883 – 89 Christmas cards survives and demonstrates the changes that have occurred in the holiday. Red and green appear with no greater frequency than other colors, and the images are more diverse. Holly branches and Santa Clauses do appear, but so do fairies, farm animals, and spring flowers.

(Clockwise from top): Aunt Evelina du Pont, grandmother Louisa Gerhard du Pont, and Louise du Pont

"As my mother was a New Yorker we always had Christmas with stockings and Christmas dinner at Winterthur, but New Year's Day was really a great day. Gentlemen of the family all paid visits in the morning bringing boxes of candy.... My aunts and uncles... and all their children stayed at Grandmama's [Eleutherian Mills]... [where there was] a large family dinner with a boiled turkey with oyster stuffing at one end of the table and a roast turkey with chestnut stuffing at the other end, and plum pudding and ice cream and everything wonderful to eat. My aunts, as had always been the custom, each took one of the window sills in the parlor to display their presents. Grandmama and my mother had a table each. It was all very festive and gay."

—Louise du Pont, from her memoir

A
Happy
Christmas.

Happy
be your
Christmas
Day

Somebody tells me,—O can it be true?—
Christmas is coming, and coming to you.
Best of good wishes I hasten to send,
Hoping God bless you, my dear little friend.

I come, a valiant chanticleer
To wish your Christmas day
Good cheer.

chapter 11

SUMMER AFTERNOONS

>>In the summertime the Winterthur estate brimmed with fruit, flowers, and friends. Cows, goats, chickens, horses, ducks, and dogs were playmates. Bicycling, canoeing, and horseback riding filled the children's days. Pauline introduced the game of croquet to Winterthur, and members of the Foster family would come down and play endless rounds of the lawn sport. "The Uncles left Friday," she wrote in 1893. "They played croquet up until the last minute."

Aside from visits with family in New York and a regular getaway to Sea Girt, New Jersey, Pauline, the Colonel, and the children rarely traveled away from Winterthur. This novelty photograph of the family posed in front of a photo backdrop of Niagara Falls probably commemorates one of these special occasions.

"*I* CAN SHUT MY EYES AND ALMOST SEE WINTERTHUR & THE LODGE & THE DRIVE THRO' THE WOODS & BROOK & PASTURE THAT WERE THE DELIGHT OF YOUR & HARRY'S HEART. I SHALL NEVER FORGET HOW YOU LOOKED THE FIRST DAY I CAME—FRESH FROM A ROMP IN THE BARN & THE SUSPICIOUS WAY YOU EYED THE NEW 'MADEMOISELLE.'"

—IDA GOEPP, THE CHILDREN'S NEW GOVERNESS, TO LOUISE DU PONT (JULY 14, 1900)

Oxen handled large farm chores.

Childhood friend Beverly Robinson, Harry and Louise's cousin, would grow up to become Harry's lawyer.

A young Marian Coffin, who would later help Harry with Winterthur's landscape design, is driving Harry's terriers, Jack and Mowgli, ca. 1900.

Baby goats were fun companions.

chapter 12

Young Harry at School

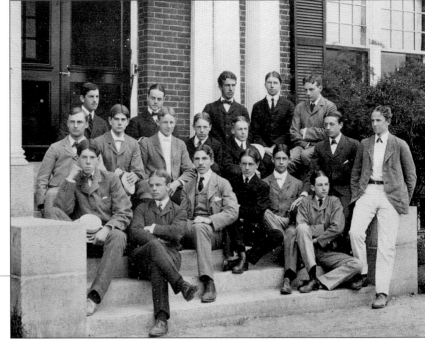

Henry Francis's class at Groton School *(he is the middle of the three boys in the row at the back on the right)*

>>At age 13, Harry was sent to Groton School as a boarder. Small for his age and used to speaking in French, not English, he missed his family and old playgrounds at Winterthur dreadfully. His parents tried to help. "I could not help thinking a great deal about you all day long. You must know how thoroughly I appreciate your feelings and how much I wish that it were in my power to make you feel immediately happy and comfortable at school!" sympathized his father. His mother sent a constant stream of cheery news about the farm and gardens. In an 1896 letter, she included three little, pressed crocus blossoms, which are still stored carefully in the Winterthur Archives:

> *My dear Harry*
> *I send you three of our little flowers that I have just brought in. The path . . . is bright yellow with the dear little crocuses. I really wish you could see them. It is real spring today and to celebrate it William has just told me that 13 little chickens are hatched, every egg came out, isn't that delightful!*

"*The* weather is beautiful today and I can see Winterthur and the flowers and everything almost as well as if I was there with you. I only wish I could be..."

—Henry Francis du Pont to his mother, Pauline (Good Friday, 1897)

Chickens at Winterthur, ca. 1900

chapter 13

LOUISE'S BUD YEAR

An array of Louise's dance cards from her "season" in New York

"DON'T YOU FEEL EXCITED ABOUT THE BRADLEY MARTIN'S BALL—I FEEL VERY MUCH SO, AND AM DYING TO HEAR ALL ABOUT YOUR DRESS... MAMA IS GOING IN WHAT COSTUME?... I IMAGINE PAPA AS SOME OLD DUKE OR SOMETHING."

—HENRY FRANCIS DU PONT TO HIS SISTER, LOUISE (FEBRUARY 8, 1897)

>>Louise's early life followed a course similar to that of many other girls of her time.

Educated at home by a succession of governesses, she made a formal debut out of the schoolroom and into society at age 16. Her first "season" was spent with her mother in a fashionable Manhattan hotel, and they were invited to an exhausting succession of afternoon teas, dances, musical evenings, and late-night balls. Louise attended the exclusive Patriarch's Ball (only progeny of the original settlers of New York were invited, and Pauline was a descendant) as well as the Bradley Martin Ball, the most extravagant private ball ever held in New York to that date. Widely debated by clergymen and journalists, the cost of the Martins' costume ball provoked weeks of interest by the press. The avalanche of adverse publicity caused the Martins to permanently abandon New York for London.

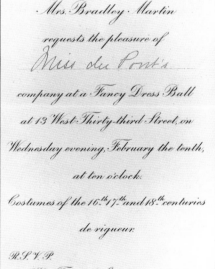

Louise's formal portrait from her debut season

Louise in her Bradley Martin Ball costume, 1897

Mrs. Bradley Martin requests the pleasure of Miss du Pont's company at a Fancy Dress Ball at 13 West Thirty-third Street, on Wednesday evening, February the tenth, at ten o'clock. Costumes of the 16th, 17th, and 18th centuries de rigueur.

R.S.V.P.
22 West Twentieth Street.

chapter 14

LOUISE'S WEDDING

*Colonel and Mrs. du Pont
have the honour of announcing
the marriage of their daughter
Louise Evelina
to
Mr. Francis Boardman Crowninshield
on Thursday, June the twenty-eighth
One thousand nine hundred
at Christ Church
Montchanin, Delaware*

>> Louise's outgoing personality flourished in the social whirl. In the spring of 1899, she became engaged, and then unengaged, to a fencing champion named J. Langdon Erving. This painful episode was made especially unpleasant by its coverage in *Town Topics*, a widely read society gossip sheet. Louise recovered from this experience with the cheerful and dignified aplomb that would characterize her life. One year later she was engaged to Francis B. Crowninshield, a well-bred Bostonian.

The rapid pace of Louise's romances did raise a few family eyebrows, though. "Aunt Vic was here this a.m. Said she had a note from Aunt Pauline announcing the engagement and in precisely the same words she did the first one!" exclaimed a cousin.

Louise and Frank's wedding at Christ Episcopal Church in Delaware took place on Thursday, June 28, 1900. The afternoon reception was a grand success, held under the tall trees on the lawns around the house at Winterthur, with Harry's pet terriers cavorting at the feet of the guests.

"I HEARD NOTHING BUT PRAISE AND COMPLIMENTS ALL DAY— ABOUT THE WAY THE PLACE LOOKED, WHAT A NICE COUPLE LOUISE AND FRANK MADE."

—BEVERLY ROBINSON, LOUISE'S COUSIN, TO PAULINE DU PONT (1900)

Louise was attended by *(from left to right)*: cousins Amy du Pont and Elaine du Pont Irving, friend Bertha King Bartlett, and cousin Pauline Robinson, all of whom carried enormous trailing bouquets of white flowers.

chapter 15

SECOND
HONEYMOON

>>In 1901 the Colonel and Pauline made their first trip back to Europe since their honeymoon. Fin-de-siècle Paris was teeming with American millionaires, and Pauline's letters to her sister back in New York indicate that they met their compatriots everywhere: at the dressmakers, at hotels, and at the great gastronomic palaces such as La Tour d' Argent, "where we ate so much that we all felt like anacondas."

Winterthur was always on Pauline's mind: a flower show at the Tuilleries was "all beautiful except the roses, with which I was disappointed, as they were not so fine as ours." The European trip seemed to spur the couple into action. Soon after they returned

The couple aboard ship bound for Europe, 1901

Pauline and the Colonel in Paris, 1901

to Delaware, they hired the architectural firm of Bissell and Perot to remodel their old home. Surviving sketches show that they planned a grand mansion for themselves, with a squash court, billiard room, second-floor music room, and an ornate summer pavilion. Winterthur would be reinvented for the 20th century.

A lighthearted moment back home at Winterthur

chapter 16

PAULINE'S DEATH

>>August of 1902 was a difficult month: the weather was "hot and foggy," the Colonel was "wretched with lumbago," and Pauline was bothered by an "absurd pain" in her side. The DuPont Company kept the Colonel busy and distracted from the house project, and Pauline had spent July preparing for the remodeling before she would go to visit Louise at Cape Cod in late August. The bothersome pain, now firmly located in Pauline's liver, became increasingly worse on this vacation. A doctor was called, but it was too late. Pauline died at her daughter's house in Marblehead on September 20, 1902.

Harry was with his mother in her last days and wrote about it in a Bible she had given him:

Wednesday September 17th
Mamma was out on the porch for half an hour in the morning. At 4:30 pm I spoke to her about Papa looking so well, and told her about progress on the house, etc. and she answered me and asked questions.

Thursday September 18th
1:30 uncle Beverly & Aunt Anna arrived Mamma's face was wreathed in smiles when she saw Uncle B. She kissed me at 1:45 and as tears were in her eyes I think she must have known the end was near.

Friday September 19th
A gleam of recognition in her eyes in the morning when I spoke to her in French. At five minutes of one she opened her eyes, I said "Well Mamma" & she said "Well dear" & when I had kissed her, kissed me. She was never conscious again after that. The last three hours before her death her breathing became very natural. It became gentler & gentler and finally stopped, at Saturday 3:30. As she lay on her death bed she looked like a young girl and had the sweetest expression, She looked so calm and happy & she knew she must be with God & the angels.

THE

HOLY BIBLE

CONTAINING THE

OLD AND NEW TESTAMENTS,

TRANSLATED OUT OF THE ORIGINAL TONGUES,
AND WITH THE FORMER TRANSLATIONS DILIGENTLY COMPARED AND REVISED,
BY HIS MAJESTY'S SPECIAL COMMAND.

Appointed to be Read in Churches.

PRINTED BY AUTHORITY.

NEW YORK BIBLE AND COMMON PRAYER BOOK SOCIETY,
12, ASTOR PLACE, NEW YORK CITY.

"*T*HIS LILY OF THE VALLEY IS THE LAST
FLOWER THAT MAMA SMELLED & REALLY
ENJOYED. FRIDAY MORNING SEPTEMBER 19."

Louise, Pauline, and Harry at Winterthur,
ca. 1900

This rose fell off Mamma's
coffin in the vestibule of the
church after the service

"*T*HIS ROSE FELL OFF MAMMA'S COFFIN
IN THE VESTIBULE OF THE CHURCH AFTER
THE SERVICE."

Life at Winterthur: A du Pont Family Album

chapter 17

FINDING SOLACE AT "THE COTTAGE"

>>The trauma of Pauline's death ran deep. Even 15 years later, the anniversary of her death could still provoke the Colonel into declaring he "did not care to live." Harry was devastated. He later said that after his mother died, he "never felt anything" again.

Abandoning his graduate school plans (he had already been accepted into the School of Practical Agriculture and Horticulture in Briarcliff Manor, New York), Harry finished his degree at Harvard and returned home to Winterthur.

"Home"—as it had been before Pauline's death—was gone. The house in which Harry had grown up was filled with workmen altering it beyond recognition. Before leaving for Cape Cod, Pauline had set up a little farmhouse for the family to live in during the remodeling. The house at the Clenny Run bridge (the current site of the Winterthur Museum Store) had been built in 1838 for Evelina and Jacques Antoine Bidermann while the big house was being built. "The Cottage" was charming, with low ceilings and big windows. Harry and his father lived there until May 1904, when the new addition to Winterthur was finally finished.

The Cottage, 1902

The Cottage living room, 1902

Building Winterthur's addition, 1902

chapter 18

A New
LIFE

A rebuilt Winterthur, 1904

>>Under the joint supervision of the grief-stricken Colonel and his son, the big house became even more grand than the couple had originally planned. The original box-shaped, Greek-revival villa was given a new, stylishly asymmetrical facade. A mansard roof, wrought-iron balconies, and patterned tiles with the du Pont coat of arms reflected the French roots of these Delaware natives. After the exterior was finished, 24-year-old Harry took control of the interior decorating—a project that would become his life's work.

A relentless perfectionist, Harry busied himself matching, ordering, and returning upholstery, furniture, carpets, and porcelains. By March 3, 1905, Harry was able to report to Louise, "I hope before long we will have the rooms finished." The care that he lavished on every detail indicates that he may have believed, as his mother's friend Edith Wharton once wrote, that "to a torn heart uncomforted by human nearness, a room may open almost human arms."

> "*I* WANT EVERYTHING DONE JUST AS IF I WERE THERE ALSO—THE SILVER SET OUT IN THE DINING ROOM EVERY DAY & PLENTY OF NICE THINGS FOR AFTERNOON TEA."
> —HENRY FRANCIS DU PONT TO AUGUST DAUPHIN, THE BUTLER (OCTOBER 2, 1911)

"The Red Room" (now the Marlborough Room) at Winterthur, ca. 1904

chapter 19

ENTERTAINING

page: 26

> "WE CAME TO AN IRON GATE WHICH SPRANG OPEN
> FOR US MYSTERIOUSLY AND AFTER WHAT SEEMED AN
> ENDLESS AVENUE THROUGH VERY TALL TREES DREW UP
> AT A HUGE PORTE COCHERE AND IN IT LOUISE WAS
> WAITING FOR ME. THE HOUSE SEEMED ENORMOUS! THE
> HALLS SOLID MARBLE WITH MARBLE PILLARS AND
> STAIRCASES WITH BRONZE RAILINGS ALL THE WAY UP TO
> THE THIRD STORY. LARGE AZALEA TREES IN FULL BLOOM
> WERE SET ABOUT IN THE HALL IN POTS."
>
> —MARIAN LAWRENCE PEABODY,
> *To Be Young Was Very Heaven* (1967)

>>The new house—with two formal parlors, a billiard room, a squash court, eight bedroom suites, and 13 servant's rooms—was perfect for entertaining. Father and son enjoyed hosting large weekend house parties, which increased in pomp after the Colonel became a Republican Senator from Delaware in 1906.

Louise's friend, Marian Lawrence Peabody, the daughter of the Episcopal Bishop of Boston, visited Winterthur in May 1905. She stayed for four days, playing bridge, canoeing, and attending the evening dinner parties:

I have two large windows in my room that open out onto a balcony and the sounds of birds and the scent of flowers that came floating in were quite intoxicating after a long northern winter. Louise's nice younger brother asked me to go on a drive and we drove for an hour or more without going off the grounds…. Shimmering white dogwood grew thick among the tall trees, and azaleas and Judas trees made a colorful underbrush. [Harry] told me to pick all the lilies of the valley I liked, write the addresses of the people to whom I wanted them sent and the butler would box and send them. This is luxury…. [Harry] is such an easy, friendly person and has a great sense of humor and is such a thoughtful host.

Canoeing on the Brandywine

Harry (*center of back row*) and friends in
front of Winterthur, March 1906

Bicycling near the Brandywine

BULLY WINTER WEEKENDS

Coaxing the horse to pull the sled at
Winterthur, March 23, 1906
(Left to right): Dorothy Welsh, C. Tiffany
Richardson, Miriam Rawson,
Anna Gerhard, Harry du Pont,
Hugh Milliken, and Helen Stockton

>> The rolling pastures and open woodlands of the Winterthur estate made it a sledding paradise in the winter. Even the most citified guests joined in the fun during snowy weekend house parties. More civilized pleasures tempered the outdoor activities: a warm bath, a roaring fire, a delicious dinner, card games, and billiards ended the days.

Thank-you notes from winter house-guests frequently express "How jolly it all was!" as Francis Chapman wrote to the Colonel after such a weekend. Or, as house-guest John Campbell White wrote to Harry in 1914, "I cannot thank you too much for a bully time last week. I always enjoy your parties and this more than any." The secluded estate grew more and more elaborate under the joint care of father and son and to most visitors, seemed a world apart.

> "THE WHOLE ATMOSPHERE OF THE PLACE, AND YOUR LIFE, IS SO UNLIKE ANYONE ELSE'S, THAT IT WAS A REAL PRIVILEGE TO BE ALLOWED TO SHARE IN IT."
>
> —MABEL CHOATE TO
> HENRY FRANCIS DU PONT (JANUARY 5, 1912)

Childhood drawing from Louise's
notebooks, 1891

Harry's cousin Elaine Irving
leads in the tobaggon. Behind her,
Dorothy Welsh, Miriam Rawson,
Helen Stockton, C. Tiffany
Richardson, and Hugh Milliken
hold on.

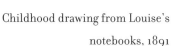

chapter 21

RUTH AND HARRY

Portrait of Ruth Wales, 1916

Portrait of Henry Francis du Pont, 1916

>>After his father became the Republican Senator from Delaware, Harry met Ruth Wales, the niece of Senator Elihu Root of New York. A talented musician and great mimic, Ruth brought a sense of fun to Harry's life. Born June 10, 1889, and raised in Southampton and Hyde Park, New York, Ruth was the pampered only child of stockbroker Edward Howe Wales and his wife, Ruth Hawks Wales.

The friendship between Harry and Ruth kindled slowly into romance. By 1914 Harry was filling Ruth's rooms with flowers. She wrote her mother that he had sent "a marvelous bunch of pink tulips.... The whole house was decorated & then he came to see me this p.m. & was furious because he had ordered lilies instead... so tonight what comes but the most enormous lot of pink lilies you ever dreamt of."

"YOU TELL ME EVERYTHING WHEN YOU SAY THAT YOUR MOTHER WOULD HAVE WANTED HER AS A DAUGHTER-IN-LAW. IT SHOWS THAT A GIRL IS A SORT TO BE A BLESSING TO A MAN WHEN HE CONNECTS HER IN HIS MIND TO HIS MOTHER."

—SHERRARD BILLING TO HENRY FRANCIS DU PONT (1916)

chapter 22

MARRIAGE TO A
MILLIONAIRE

"More than a few of her contemporaries reminded Ruth Wales, now Mrs. Henry Francis du Pont, at her wedding at Hyde Park last Saturday of the many times she had expressed herself as being absolutely unchangeable in her determination never to marry. She took the chaffing in good part, for she had been very frank, during the weeks preceding her wedding, in confessing that she was terribly in love. Therefore being a very happy bride, she was also a very pretty one, wearing a rose-point veil that had belonged to her grandmother, Mrs. Salem H. Wales, who was also Mrs. Elihu Root's mother. Few brides ever received so many diamonds."

—from *Town Topics,* June 29, 1916

Mr. and Mrs. Edward Howe Wales

request the honour of

Mrs Walsh's

presence at the marriage of their daughter

Ruth

to

Mr. Henry Francis du Pont

on Saturday, the twenty-fourth of June

at half after four o'clock

at Saint James's Church

Hyde Park-on-the-Hudson, New York

>>After their long courtship, Ruth and Harry's engagement was brief. On May 8, 1916, Harry asked Ruth to be his wife, and six weeks later, on June 24, 1916, the couple were married at the Wales's home in Hyde Park, New York. Harry and his father spent the night before the ceremony at the home of Harry's schoolmate Franklin Delano Roosevelt, then secretary of the Navy. A private train was hired to take the guests from New York City to Hyde Park. Roosevelt must have added a great deal of dash to the event when he sped up the Hudson River from Manhattan to Hyde Park in a government torpedo boat. Newspapers ranging from the *New York Times* to the local *Poughkeepsie Press* regaled their readers with all the nuptial details, from the

Ruth arriving at the ceremony

"DEAR RUTH AND HARRY, I HAVE BEEN WANTING TO WRITE TO YOU BOTH TO TELL YOU HOW MUCH I ENJOYED YOUR BEAUTIFUL WEDDING.... THE ROSES WERE LOVELY, AND THEIR PERFUME DELICIOUS AND THE LITTLE BAY TREES LINKED WITH RIBBON MADE A CHARMING LITTLE LANE DOWN WHICH YOU WALKED. THE BRIDE'S DRESS I THOUGHT MOST ARTISTIC AND BEAUTIFUL WITH ITS SHIMMERING SILVER AND RARE LACE."

—EVELINA DU PONT, HARRY'S AUNT (JULY 11, 1916)

number of the bride's attendants (none) to the number of the groom's (seven) to a complete list of the wedding presents.

chapter 23

WINTERTHUR'S NEW MISTRESS

Harry and Ruth at Winterthur, ca. 1918

>>The newlyweds returned from their cross-country honeymoon in late September 1916, and Ruth took over as mistress of Winterthur—the first since Pauline's death 14 years before. Ruth understood that it was not going to be easy to find her place in this well-established, masculine household. While still engaged, she had written to the Colonel, "I do hope that you will not find it trying to have me in the house at Winterthur, and please believe me, dear Colonel du Pont, that I shall try always to do my best in every respect."

Retired from the United States Senate only a few months after Ruth and Harry's wedding, the Colonel spent his days working with his son on ambitious plans for Winterthur, which had grown to about 1,446 acres. The estate supported a post office, a railway stop, and a self-sufficient farm system with a butcher shop, a dairy, a sawmill, and a tannery. The cow breeding project escalated in 1916 as other improvements were made to the grounds and gardens. Ninety workers' cottages surrounded the main house, and according to Louise's friend Marian Lawrence Peabody, "There were two or three hundred working on the place all the time, doing and undoing the orders of the Colonel.... a terrace of solid masonry [was built] and then the Colonel decided it would look better a few inches to the right or left so they'd do it all over again."

REGISTERED HOLSTEIN CATTLE

EXPRESS
CHANIN.
AWARE

TELEGRAMS
TELEPHONE OL 2-49
WILMINGTON

WINTERTHUR FARMS

WINTERTHUR, DELAWARE

View of Winterthur with cows grazing
on the meadow

"*T*HE BEAUTIFUL HOME WILL HAVE, FROM ALL I HEAR, A MOST ATTRACTIVE AND FITTING CHATELAINE! I REMEMBER ONCE YOUR MOTHER SAYING SHE WISHED SHE COULD LOOK IN THE FUTURE & SEE WHO YOU WOULD BRING INTO THE HOME. HOW THOROUGHLY SHE WOULD HAVE REJOICED IN THIS HAPPY CONSUMATION."

—AMY BARTLETT, A FRIEND OF PAULINE DU PONT'S, TO HENRY FRANCIS DU PONT (1916)

chapter 24

THE
KITTY

>>On April 30, 1918, Harry and Ruth welcomed their first child, Pauline Louise. Named after both the Colonel's beloved wife and daughter, she was a beautiful and abundantly healthy baby.

Ruth and Harry with baby
Pauline Louise, 1918

> *T*HE KITTY IS TOO LOVELY, SLEEPS SO WELL & IS <u>SO</u> BRIGHT. I SING TO HER AND SHE JOINS IN ALWAYS. LAUGHS AND TALKS ALL HER WAKING MOMENTS."
>
> —RUTH DU PONT TO HER MOTHER,
> RUTH HAWKS WALES (JULY 2, 1918)

Pauline Louise playing in Winterthur's gardens, 1920

chapter 25

THE
MONKEY

Pauline Louise, Harry, and Ruth with the new baby, Ruth Ellen, 1922

>>Life in a house run for the comfort of a man in his seventies became increasingly difficult with a new baby. The time Ruth could spend alone with her husband was minimal and precious. To the dismay of the Colonel, Ruth and Harry bought an apartment in New York in 1921. Here they could entertain more freely and Ruth could be closer to her mother. On January 14, 1922, their second daughter, Ruth Ellen, was born. Ruth wrote to her mother about their namesake, calling her "the dearest monkey."

Sisters Pauline Louise and Ruth Ellen, 1922

Ruth Ellen and
Pauline Louise,
ca. 1924

"*L*AST NIGHT LITTLE H [HARRY] & I TOOK OUR SUPPER IN A BASKET & STARTED DRIVING SOON AFTER 5, WENT ALL AROUND THE BRANDYWINE, ATE IN THE WOODS & RETURNED AT DARK. IT WAS HEAVENLY. . ."

—RUTH DU PONT TO HER MOTHER,
RUTH HAWKS WALES (JULY 1, 1918)

chapter 26

The BIRDS

Henry Francis and Ruth du Pont with daughters
Pauline Louise and Ruth Ellen, ca. 1924

>>Throughout the early 1920s, Harry and his family divided their time between the New York apartment, a Southampton summerhouse, a Florida winter retreat, and the Winterthur estate. They returned to visit the Colonel regularly, on spring and fall weekends and holidays. Despite living in so many places, or perhaps because of this factor, life quickly settled into a well-

"WE HAD A PERFECT P.M. YESTERDAY. TOOK THE BIRDS [PAULINE AND RUTH] TO SEE THE COWS & CALVES, THEN TO GATHER WILD STRAWBERRIES. HAD A LOVELY RIDE ALONG THE BRANDYWINE."
—RUTH DU PONT TO HER MOTHER, RUTH HAWKS WALES (JUNE 11, 1925)

established routine, with a predictable and seasonal cycle of movement among the houses.

The Delaware estate was the hub. This primacy was expressed in many ways, even in the food the family ate. Beef, lamb, pork, chicken, turkey, guinea fowl, duck, and vegetables were specially packed at the Winterthur farm and sent by train to the family kitchens in Long Island, Florida, and New York City. The Delaware estate and the bounty of its land was the anchor of their lives.

Spring vacation in Boca Grande, Florida, ca. 1926

Equestrians extraordinaire, Ruth Ellen
and Pauline Louise, 1927

DEAR
MISS YOU SO
MUCH
I HOPE
YOU ARE
INJOUING
THE SNOU

Note from Ruth Ellen to her father

Life at Winterthur: A du Pont Family Album

chapter 27

THE COLONEL'S DEATH

>>The Colonel was vigorous right up to the end of his long life. In his seventies he continued to ride horses around his estate, he published three books, and he helped Louise restore his childhood home, Eleutherian Mills, in "period style." His love for children seemed only to increase over the years. At Christmas dinner, young family members vied to be seated next to the sometimes intimidating old man because he always shared his strawberries.

Louise and Harry were at his bedside when he died peaceably and without pain early on December 31, 1926. He was a senator, author, and recipient of the Congressional Medal of Honor, but perhaps his most enduring legacy was the deep sense of civic responsibility, especially in respect to the preservation of history, that he instilled in both his children. The son, whose household title changed from Mr. Harry to Mr. du Pont upon his father's death, was now master of the estate.

"THE TREES HAVE BEEN COVERED WITH THE MOST WONDERFUL DECORATIONS IN ICE, WHICH MADE THE WOODS LOOK LIKE A FAIRY LAND. I AM GLAD THE CHILDREN WERE HERE TO SEE IT. IT IS AN INCIDENT IN THEIR YOUNG LIVES WHICH THEY WILL PROBABLY NEVER FORGET."

—HENRY ALGERNON DU PONT TO HIS DAUGHTER, LOUISE, FOUR DAYS BEFORE HIS DEATH

Colonel Henry Algernon du Pont, ca. 1920

Ruth du Pont at the Colonel's grave

Condolence note sent with flowers from the White House

chapter 28

A New
WINTERTHUR

>>Harry began redecorating Winterthur immediately after the death of the Colonel. A plan for a serious rebuilding of the house was afoot by the fall of 1928; it called for an additional 130 rooms. The new wing, designed by Albert Ely Ives, was intended to house the antique American furniture and architecture that Harry had been collecting and storing in the barns.

While the house was under construction, the family lived in the same little Clenny Run cottage that Pauline had arranged during the 1902 renovation. In her 1999 memoir, *Henry F. du Pont and Winterthur*, Ruth Ellen wrote of her affection for life in that little house, "cozy with chintz, firelight and tiny bedrooms," and about the construction going on around her: "The maze of roughly plastered corridors and wet cement through which my father often led us was not encouraging."

Winterthur before construction, July 15, 1929

Construction under way, November 15, 1929

Work continues, March 24, 1930

The new Winterthur

chapter 29

Fantastical
Vision

Enjoying the pool, May 1935

>>On April 1, 1931, the family moved into the enlarged house, and, after an initial feeling of disorientation, the family really began "enjoying life," according to Ruth. The girls were installed in a homey set of rooms on the third floor. Ruth's suite was to the north and Harry's to the south. There were 15 bedrooms in all, not including the 23 servants rooms. Downstairs, the sumptuous American interiors for which Winterthur would become famous had begun to take shape. Silver, paintings, textiles, porcelains,

a private movie theater provided a surplus of entertainment for rainy days. Outdoors were the heated swimming pool, croquet and tennis courts, and acres of beautiful gardens designed by Marian Coffin.

Built during the height of the Great Depression, Harry's fantastical vision of Winterthur as a treasury of Americana kept many families solvent in the 1930s. New gardens and a professional golf course were added at the same time the house was enlarged, and in the middle of all this activity, the great cow barn burned down and had to be rebuilt. "Because of Harry du Pont, I had no depression," New York antique textiles dealer Elinor Merrill stated simply. Constructions crews, architects, landscapers, engineers, gardeners, upholsterers, locksmiths, electricians, plumbers, painters, golf pros, and an assorted group of merchants were also able to get their families through those hard times thanks to Harry's pursuit of perfection.

> "*T*HE POOL WAS HEAVENLY THIS A.M. WE HAD LUNCH ON THE NEW PORCH OVERLOOKING THE GARDEN & IT WAS A GRAND SUCCESS. I MUST SAY HOUSE & GARDENS ARE DREAMS OF BEAUTY."
>
> —RUTH DU PONT TO HER MOTHER, RUTH HAWKS WALES (MAY 1931)

and furniture from the 17th, 18th, and 19th centuries were arranged in rooms lined with compatible architecture. But there was more than antique furniture to keep guests and family amused. A bowling alley, a ping-pong room, and a badminton court that doubled as

Bird's-eye view of Winterthur with the
new wing, after 1930.

A day of tennis, May 1935

Relaxing on the terrace after a long day
of games, May 1935

A golf outing, May 1935

Life at Winterthur: A du Pont Family Album

chapter 30

Weekends at
Winterthur

Chrysanthemum tree in the conservatory at Winterthur

Houseguests at Winterthur, 1935

Tea in the conservatory, 1935

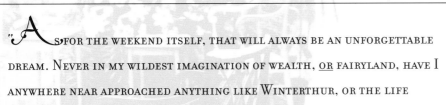

"As for the weekend itself, that will always be an unforgettable dream. Never in my wildest imagination of wealth, <u>or</u> fairyland, have I anywhere near approached anything like Winterthur, or the life there. And the thing that impressed me as much as the luxury, if not more, was the utter simplicity and warmth of the people. Mr. du Pont, whom I had met once for lunch at the Colony Club immediately after we were married, greeted me as if he had known me all my life and was especially fond of me.... I have always felt completely at ease with Mrs. du Pont, but she couldn't have greeted her daughters more warmly. We arrived around six o'clock and after a preliminary wash-up in a marble lavatory near the front door, she started to lead me into the large living room at the foot of the beautiful staircase by the conservatory for tea with the other house guests. I say started because it was a long trip. The first thing that met my eye, way ahead of me, was a floor to ceiling cascade of the most gorgeous chrysanthemums, gold and white and flame. I stopped dead in my tracks and must have looked like a fool with my mouth open—and as I stood breathless at this beauty way ahead of me, my eye was caught by something beside me. I looked around at the room I was in,—and Mrs. du Pont burst out laughing! I just gasped! It was the Chinese room—the huge room with the big fireplace and the unbelievable Chinese scenic paper on the walls—and everywhere in every flat space big enough to hold a vase of flowers: Huge crystal bowls of pure white chrysanthemums; bowls of the most delicate, pink chrysanthemums; tiny vases with a single hibiscus—three or four of these on a single table. I was wordless—indeed breathless—and Mrs. du Pont was sweet enough to know how I felt because she just let me stand and drink it in.... Mrs. du Pont finally maneuvered me into the room where tea was served and where Fran was already comfortably seated and I met the other house guests.... After tea, Mrs. du Pont took us to our rooms to dress for dinner—and again I was shocked into speechlessness. We had the suite of rooms next to hers—a bedroom for Fran with a bath, and an enormous bedroom for me with a bath that I would have been perfectly content to spend the weekend in, and lit by dozens of what I thought were candles—it took me a full hour to wake up to the fact that they were tiny electric light bulbs in the shape of a candle flame. My clothes were all unpacked and hung up, my toilet articles arranged in the bathroom.... Getting dressed was quite a process, what with so much to look at and luxuriate in and gasp at—even to a card on which to order breakfast."

—Mrs. Francis Woodbridge

Life at Winterthur: A du Pont Family Album

chapter 31

Shifting of the
Vessels

"You ask me for the menu of my party: clear soup, lobster mayonnaise, duckling & veg. & caramel icecream, & a big birthday cake. We were to have a beet salad vinaigrette but Miss Ward [the housekeeper] forgot to put it on the cook's menu and it was just as well, as the dinner was long enough as it was."

—Ruth Wales du Pont to her mother, Ruth Hawks Wales

(June 12, 1931)

>> Harry invested huge amounts of time, thought, and money in his table settings. A quiet man who loved playing host, he kept careful records of the flower, vase, china, silver, glass, and linen combinations that he, and his butler, dreamed up.

Individually, the lists read almost like poetry:

"pink gallanthus orchids in Norwegian silver beakers, pastel poppies, mauve thalictrum with purple Staffordshire china and mauve edge doilies."

This level of attention was not always easy on the staff. Ruth used to tell a story about a maid who gave notice right after she successfully finished Harry's demanding table-waiting training. When asked why she was leaving so soon, the maid answered shortly: "Too much shifting of the vessels for the fewness of the victuals!"

A typical table arrangement by Harry for a dinner (this one from the 1960s), photo by Peter Pagan

chapter 32

GROWING UP AT
WINTERTHUR

>>Although they went to school in New York and later Virginia, Pauline and Ruth were at Winterthur often enough to get to know the other children who lived on the estate. Jane and Emily Norris, two of the postmistress's children, were around the same age as Ruth, and they all played together, roaming over the estate. As Jane later recalled:

Ruth Ellen was a great tree climber. I think we have climbed every tree around

Pauline Louise and Ruth Ellen, ca. 1930

Harry, Ruth Ellen, Ruth, and Pauline Louise on a family vacation in California, May 1936

Formal portrait of Pauline Louise and Ruth Ellen, 1935

here. Now Pauline Louise was a little more reserved wasn't she? She played tennis with us. She had a governess who was very fussy when she was smaller and I think she wasn't allowed to climb trees or anything like that.

"THE ENTERTAINER WAS A GREAT SUCCESS... HE DID SOME EXCEL-LENT MAGIC AS WELL AS JUGGLING AND THE CHILDREN WERE ROARING WITH LAUGHTER. THE SUPPER TABLE LOOKED LOVELY, AND THE MEAL WAS GOOD. SUCH A PRETTY CAKE ALL DECORATED WITH PINK AND GREEN, AND THE JACK HORNER PIE MADE A GREAT HIT. WE HAD 24 CHILDREN. RE ENJOYED IT ENORMOUSLY AND PL WAS A CHARMING HOSTESS. ALL THE CHILDREN BEHAVED, AND EVERY-THING WENT OFF WITHOUT A HITCH."

—RUTH WALES DU PONT TO HER MOTHER, RUTH HAWKS WALES (MAY 1, 1924)

chapter 33

PAULINE'S COMING OUT PARTY

Pauline Louise, 1935

>>Pauline Louise's coming out party was held at Winterthur on June 26, 1935. Considered with as much care as the Colonel would have run a military operation, plans and counterplans for the party were outlined in countless lists and memos.

Ultimately, things worked out perfectly.

In case of rain, Harry had decorated a tent and 500 umbrellas with balloons and flowers. At one point during the clear, starry night, he led his friend Mrs. Bertha Rose away from the party.

"Come and look at this" he said, and they walked to the other side of the green. "Here," Mrs. Rose recalled, "was this great, empty tent, all perfectly beautiful, just because it didn't rain."

"I HAVE NEVER SEEN ANYTHING IN THE MOVIES THAT RIVALED IT. YOU KNOW, THEY HAD COLORED LIGHTS HIGH IN THE TREES AND COLORED BALLOONS ALL UP IN THE TREES."

—MRS. WALTER HECKMAN, FROM ORAL HISTORY PROJECT (TAPED JULY 19, 1973)

The swimming pool decorated for the party, 1935

Party tents (in case of rain)

chapter 34

PAULINE'S WEDDING

Pauline Louise Harrison and Alfred Craven Harrison,
January 15, 1938

>>Almost 1,000 people were invited to the wedding of Pauline Louise du Pont and Alfred Craven Harrison, and the party was arranged in less than two months. Harry marshaled his forces once more and planned the perfect day. Eight hundred and thirty-five guests attended the celebration that unexpectedly warm and sunny January day. So many arrived from New York that special arrangements had to be made at the Wilmington train station.

"*I* WANT TO TELL YOU ABOUT PAULINE'S ENGAGEMENT TO ALFRED HARRISON OF PHILADELPHIA. HE IS A YOUNG LAWYER 27 YEARS OLD, TALL AND DARK, HAS A VERY GOOD SENSE OF HUMOR AND PLAYS ALL GAMES PASSABLY. HIS FATHER AND MOTHER ARE GREAT FRIENDS OF OURS WHOM WE HAVE KNOWN FOREVER WHICH MAKES IT ALL VERY CONGENIAL. THEY ARE GOING TO BE MARRIED ON THE 15TH OF JANUARY AND I DO HOPE WE WILL NOT HAVE A HORRIBLE BLIZZARD JUST AT THAT TIME."

—HENRY FRANCIS DU PONT TO HIS FRIEND
BARON RENÉ DE STAEL (NOVEMBER 16, 1937)

The wedding party assembling
in the Chinese Parlor

Mr. & Mrs. Henry Francis du Pont
request the honour of your presence
at the marriage of their daughter
Pauline Louise
and
Mr. Alfred Craven Harrison
Saturday afternoon January the fifteenth
nineteen hundred and thirty-eight
at quarter past three o'clock
Christ Church, Christiana Hundred
Delaware

"All I remember about Pauline Louise's wedding were masses of flowers up and down the stairs and flowers all along, you know, like a frieze all along the room as you went in to shake hands... I remember the flowers. You could walk on them there were so many."

—Mrs. Bertha Rose, from oral history project (taped December 13, 1973)

Dancing in the Montmorenci Stair Hall

Pauline and Alfred's wedding cake

chapter 35

RUTH'S
COMING OUT
PARTY

Mr. and Mrs. Henry Francis du Pont
request the pleasure of

company at dinner in honour of
Miss Ruth Ellen du Pont
on Wednesday, the thirteenth of September
at half after eight o'clock
Winterthur

>> Ruth Ellen's coming out party was held at Winterthur on September 13, 1939. The counterplans for Ruth's debut were on a different order of magnitude from her sister's. War was looming, and everyone knew life was going to be very different soon.

Herald Tribune

SUNDAY, AUGUST 13, 1939

in Newport and the Hamptons at Peak of Season

Ruth's coming out party was not photographed, but her debut was well publicized in the society pages. (*Ruth is at the far right.*)

"DUE TO THE UNSETTLED WORLD CONDITIONS, I WANT TO ADVISE YOU, IN CASE THERE IS A WORLD WAR AND ALL DEBUTANTE PARTIES ARE GIVEN UP, WE OF COURSE SHALL HAVE TO CANCEL OUR ARRANGEMENTS FOR THE DANCE FOR OUR DAUGHTER ON THE 13TH OF SEPTEMBER, BUT WE EARNESTLY HOPE SUCH WILL NOT BE THE CASE."

—HENRY FRANCIS DU PONT
TO THE CATERER (AUGUST 1939)

"WE GAVE A VERY SUCCESSFUL COMING OUT PARTY FOR RUTH ELLEN ON SEPTEMBER 13... THE DANCING TENT WAS A PALE PINK AND THE FLOOR WAS A MOST BEAUTIFUL FUSCHIA RED WITH A PAINTED PINK SCALLOPED BORDER. THE WALK FROM THE CONSERVATORY TO THE DANCING TENT WAS LINED WITH PALE BLUE SILK AND I HAD ABOUT TWENTY PEACH TREES ALONG THE WALK, WITH THE MOST COLOSSAL PEACHES ON THEM YOU EVER SAW IN YOUR LIFE. IT WAS REALLY QUITE RAVISHING."

—HENRY FRANCIS DU PONT TO
MARIAN COFFIN (NOVEMBER 29, 1939)

chapter 36

The
1940s

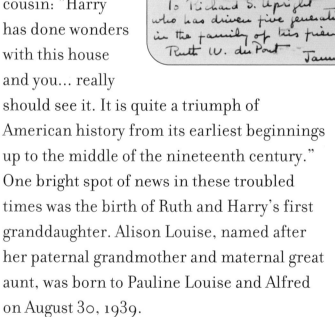

To Richard S. Upright —
who has driven five generations
in the family of his friend
Ruth W. du Pont   January, 1940

Chauffeur Richard S. Upright, Pauline Louise with baby Alison,
and Ruth du Pont, 1940

>>The threat of world war stepped up the building plans at Winterthur. Ruth explained her husband's frantic activities to a cousin: "Harry has done wonders with this house and you... really should see it. It is quite a triumph of American history from its earliest beginnings up to the middle of the nineteenth century." One bright spot of news in these troubled times was the birth of Ruth and Harry's first granddaughter. Alison Louise, named after her paternal grandmother and maternal great aunt, was born to Pauline Louise and Alfred on August 30, 1939.

As predicted, the declaration of war slowed everything down. All the young men left the estate, and food and gasoline were rationed. No new building was done at Winterthur during the war, but the day after peace was declared, Harry assembled his employees. "The War's over—let's get started," said the boss.

chapter 37

RUTH'S
WEDDING

Ruth Ellen's bridal portrait, 1947

>>Nine-hundred people were invited to Ruth and George Lord Jr.'s post-nuptial afternoon tea at Winterthur on March 22, 1947. Harry worried about the weather and considered every detail of the wedding, from the figures on the cake to the type of supplies needed for the guest bathrooms. The throng toasted the newlyweds and nibbled at the chicken croquettes, fruit salad, tea sandwiches, and little cakes. Almost all who were invited came, many for a last peek at the house before it would become a museum. Like the Colonel and Pauline before them, Harry and Ruth were planning a major reinvention of Winterthur following their daughter's wedding.

"*T*HE WEDDING WENT OFF WITH GREAT SUCCESS. THERE WERE OVER A THOUSAND PEOPLE HERE AND THEY DRANK THIRTY CASES OF CHAMPAGNE. RUTH ELLEN LOOKED VERY LOVELY AND PAULINE ALSO WITH A YELLOW DRESS AND CARRYING A BOUQUET OF MOSTLY YELLOW PANSIES. RUTH ELLEN WORE PL'S WEDDING DRESS OF WHITE SATIN MATERIAL AND HAD SOME OF LOUISE'S LACE ON HER VEIL. SHE HAD A LARGE BOUQUET OF PHALAAENOPSIS ORCHIDS WHICH CAME FROM PS'S GREENHOUSES. MY RUTH LOOKED HER VERY BEST IN A BEIGE DRESS."

—HENRY FRANCIS DU PONT TO BARON RENÉ DE STAEL
(JANUARY 15, 1947)

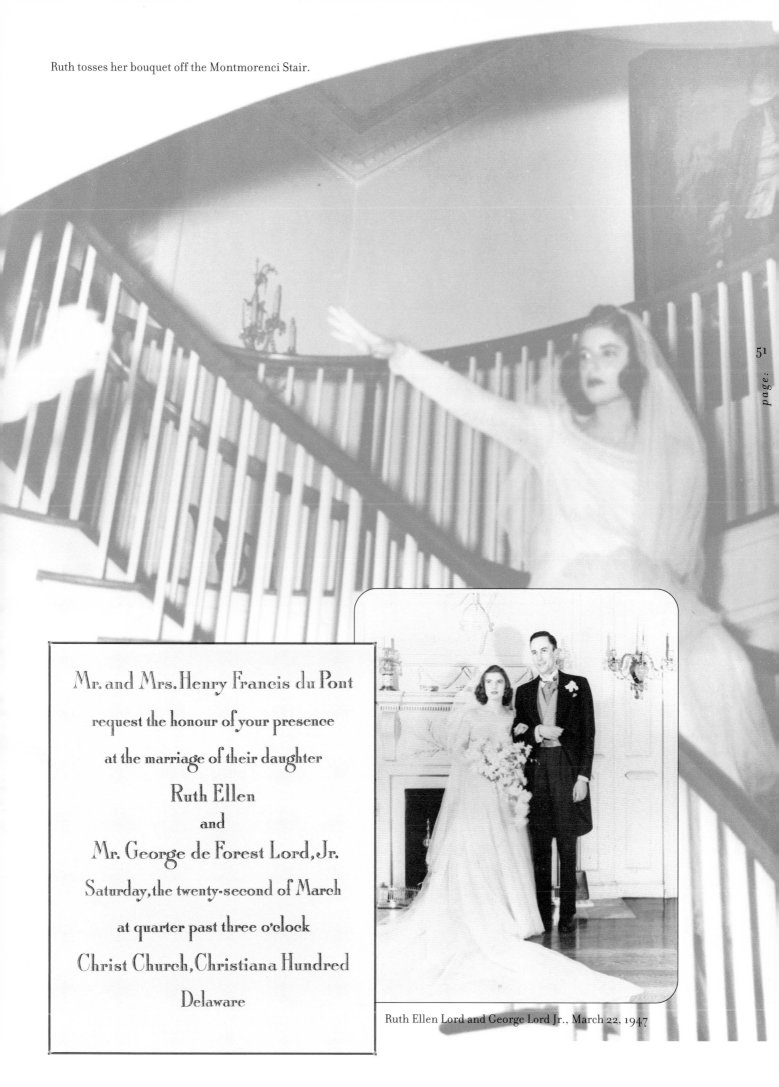

Ruth tosses her bouquet off the Montmorenci Stair.

Mr. and Mrs. Henry Francis du Pont
request the honour of your presence
at the marriage of their daughter
Ruth Ellen
and
Mr. George de Forest Lord, Jr.
Saturday, the twenty-second of March
at quarter past three o'clock
Christ Church, Christiana Hundred
Delaware

Ruth Ellen Lord and George Lord Jr., March 22, 1947

Life at Winterthur: A du Pont Family Album

chapter 38

POSTSCRIPT

Henry Francis du Pont in his garden at Winterthur, ca. 1950

>>On January 18, 1951, a small party was held at the Winterthur house. There were drinks on the dining room porch, a delicious meal served by footmen, and so many flowers on the table the guests couldn't see the person seated across from them. There was a difference to this party, it was the absolute last private party at Winterthur. Harry and Ruth would be leaving for a Florida trip, and the house would become a museum. The day before, Harry had written a rather poignant letter to a friend: "Tomorrow I leave Winterthur forever."

During the evening, while the guests talked and laughed and Harry puffed on his special monogrammed gold-tipped cigarettes, the hall below was filled with Ruth and Harry's suitcases. The family had to be out of the house at midnight, and the family did indeed leave the Winterthur house forever. The Cottage on Clenny Run, torn down and rebuilt from scratch, would serve as their Winterthur residence for the rest of their lives.

> "*O*UR NEW HOUSE IS SWEET AND NOT TOO BIG, AND I THINK IF WE EVER GET SETTLED, WE WILL BE VERY HAPPY IN IT. AT PRESENT THE HOUSE IS FULL OF WORKMEN, DUST, NOISE AND CONFUSION."
>
> —RUTH DU PONT TO MISS PEARSON (NOVEMBER 19, 1951)